STOICISM

THE PHILOSOPHY OF CALMNESS

WRITTEN BY

George Muntau

© Copyright 2017 by George Muntau - All rights reserved.

The following book is reproduced below with the goal of providing information that is as accurate and as reliable as possible. Regardless, purchasing this book can be seen as consent to the fact that both the publisher and the author of this book are in no way experts on the topics discussed within, and that any recommendations or suggestions made herein are for entertainment purposes only. Professionals should be consulted as needed before undertaking any of the action endorsed herein.

This declaration is deemed fair and valid by both the American Bar Association and the Committee of Publishers Association and is legally binding throughout the United States.

Furthermore, the transmission, duplication or reproduction of any of the following work, including precise information, will be considered an illegal act, irrespective whether it is done electronically or in print. The legality extends to creating a secondary or tertiary copy of the work or a recorded copy and is only allowed with express written consent of the Publisher. All additional rights are reserved.

The information in the following pages is broadly considered to be a truthful and accurate account of facts, and as such any inattention, use or misuse of the information in question by the reader will render any resulting actions solely under their purview. There are no scenarios in which the publisher or the original author of this work can be in any fashion deemed liable for any hardship or damages that may befall them after undertaking information described herein.

Additionally, the information found on the following pages is intended for informational purposes only and should thus be considered, universal. As befitting its nature, the information presented is without assurance regarding its continued validity or interim quality. Trademarks that mentioned are done without written consent and can in no way be considered an endorsement from the trademark holder.

TABLE OF CONTENTS

Introduction 5
Chapter One: Historical Background And Foundation Of Stoicism.. 7
Chapter Two: Greek Stoicism 20
Chapter Three: Stoicism In Rome 25
Chapter Four: Neuroplasticity 30
Chapter Five: Understanding Emotions 34
Chapter Six: Stoicism And Free Will 40
Chapter Seven: Stoicism And Modern Life 45
Conclusion 62

INTRODUCTION

Philosophy is not implied as a simple theoretical regulation of life, but an applicable one. It should enable you to carry on with a productive and worthy life here on Earth. It is in some ways a manual to live, one that has been laid out and refined by a portion of the preeminent pioneers in history. I'm certain we would all be able to identify with the inquiry of ourselves "What is an ideal approach to live?" As I discussed in a past post, living without lament is a focal occupant keeping in mind the end goal to accomplish a level of fulfillment toward the finish of life. Philosophy can give us the principles to guarantee that we achieve that state.

One particular philosophy that can provide us with these principles is Stoicism.

Interest for Stoicism has encountered a renaissance as of late. However, in spite of the expanding notoriety of this old philosophy, confusions persist about it. For instance, many individuals assume that to be Stoic implies not feeling or expressing any feelings, including delight, and that Stoicism expects one to carry on with an insipid and austere way of life. In this book, we share the inceptions of Stoicism and how the Romans adjusted Greek Stoicism to fit their way of life. We then get into particular Stoic practices you can execute today to begin enhancing your life.

In case you've been wanting to comprehend Stoicism all the more, yet haven't known how to begin, this book is an extraordinary presentation and is pressed with not just a simple foundation data but rather noteworthy counsel.

CHAPTER ONE

HISTORICAL BACKGROUND AND FOUNDATION OF STOICISM

I. HISTORY

Stoicism is a Hellenistic (developed by the Hellenistic civilization following Aristotle) philosophy that draws focus to personal ethics based on a system of logic and perception of the natural world. In depth, Stoicism asserts that judgment should not be based on one's speech or words but rather their actions. This philosophy originated from and was founded by Zeno of Citium from Athens which today is Cyprus in 300 BC and was practiced famously by Seneca, Epictetus and Marcus Aurelius who were its three principal leaders. When Nero turned against Seneca and demanded his suicide, Seneca proceeded to provide solace to his wife and friends. Epictetus, on the other hand, withstood the horrors of slavery and eventually began his school where he taught many brilliant Romans. Marcus Aurelius, who was the Roman Emperor, wrote himself notes every day about humility, restraint, and compassion.

Socrates was one of the biggest influencers of Stoicism. Like many philosophies, Stoicism is a variation of other philosophies, and Zeno's ideas were obtained from the Cynics. Cynicism was founded by Antisthenes, who was a disciple of Socrates.

Its name, a derivative of Stoa Poikile, "the painted porch," was a Stoics open market and they would meet to teach and discuss philosophy. Unlike other schools of thought and philosophy, Zeno, its founder, taught Stoicism in public at around the beginning of 301 BC. Stoicism became the most popular and foremost philosophy amongst the educated (and) elite in Rome and thrived under the Roman Empire. However, Chrysippus, Zeno's most influential student, is credited for modeling Stoicism as we know it today. Stoicism is divided by scholars into three phases: Early Stoa, the Middle Stoa, and the Late Stoa.

II. PHILOSOPHICAL PRECURSORS

Stoicism is a Greek eudemonic reasoning, which implies that we can anticipate that it will be impacted by its prompt antecedents and counterparts, and also to openly be in basic exchange with both. They incorporate Socratic ways, which have touched base with us mostly early using the Dispassionate discourse; the Scholarly institution embraced Platonism, especially during the Distrustful stage; the Peripatetic school took up Aristotelianism; Negativity; Wariness; as well as Luxury. Significantly, keep minding the end goal that sets a quantitative investigation through placing things in a setting, and the investigation of surviving track records of known rationalists belonging to the antiquated Greco-Roman world (Goulet 2013), gauges at the time, the main schools needed diving request: Stoics (12%), Scholastics Platonists (19%), Peripatetic-Aristotelians (6%) and Epicureans (8%).

Eudemonia implied an existence that warranted living, frequently deciphered these days as "satisfaction" in the wide sense, or all the more fittingly, prosperity. According to Greco-Romans, it frequently included (yet contrary) the magnificence of moral ethics as a major characteristic. Subsequently, the idea is firmly identified with that of upright morals. Broadie and Rowe (2002), borrowed from the Nicomachean Morals by Aristotle as there's a broad connection and resuscitated to current circumstances by various rationalists.

The best way to comprehend stoicism with regards to the distinctions among a portion of the schools compared at the time. Taking an instance of Socrates' contention in the Euthydemus, that ethical-ness, and specifically, the four cardinal excellences of shrewdness, valor, equity, and balance, are the main great. Everything else is neither great nor terrible all by itself. By differentiating, for Aristotle the ethics (of which he recorded an astounding twelve) were important, however, not adequate for eudaimonia. One likewise required a specific level of positive merchandise, for example, well-being, riches, training, and even a touch of good looks. At the end of the day, Aristotle explained the fairly commonsensical idea that to prosper in life, it is partly exertion, since an individual is able and should develop character, as well as partly luckiness, as both the social and physical attributes that model a person's life.

Complexity, addressing the somewhat extraordinary (at the time notwithstanding) Skeptics' opinion, whose imagination was not just prudence being the main great, similar to Socrates, however, that the extra products that Aristotle was stressed over were diversions and should have been decidedly kept away. Diogenes of Sinope was a celebrated skeptic. The celebration of such skeptics' austere and perhaps diverse way of living, was encapsulated by Diogenes Laertius in an anecdote about Diogenes of Sinope. "One day, watching a youngster drinking out of his hands, he cast away the glass from his wallet with the words, 'A tyke has beaten me in modesty of living.'"

The Aristotelian is regarded to be an aristocratic approach: in a scenario where one's life lacks certain privileges, attaining eudaimonia is impossible.

When you look at it from a different angle, the Cynics used to live the real form of minimalistic lifestyle, which a normal human being cannot practice. The Stoics tried in the past to live a combination of both sides of life, opting to live the twin crucial ideas. They speak of virtue as the only true way to understand eudemonia irrespective of someone's condition. Education, health, and wealth are preferred or not preferred, just like when you consider ignorance, poverty, and sickness. With that in mind, do not confuse them with valuable things.

III. ARGUMENTS WITH OTHER HELLENISTIC PHILOSOPHIES

One ought to comprehend the advancement of every single Greek school of theory similar to the consequence of consistent exchange among themselves, a discourse that frequently prompted incomplete modifications of positions inside whichever school, or the changing of an idea from a different school that had been selected according to Gill, 2003. In order to perceive the unraveling of this according to Stoicism, a couple of cases can be considered, identified with the connections amongst both Luxury and Stoicism, Platonism, and Aristotelianism, having not overlooked immediately the impact of Negativity on the very birth of Stoicism as well as the distance to Epictetus.

Truly, Epictetus is unequivocal regarding his—negative—sentiments about Epicureans, bringing out a cut out difference as conceivable as a comparison of the last's worry of joy, torment and the Stoic concentrate on righteousness and character that possesses honesty. AS an example, Talks I.23 is entitled "Against Epicurus," which starts: "[1] Even Epicurus understands that we are social animals by nature, however, once he has recognized our greatness with the shell, he can't state anything conflicting with that. [2] For he additionally demands—appropriately—that we should not regard or affirm anything that is not agreeable with the great." The Epicureans emphasize that the delight and nonappearance of agony in the body "The shell" is what prompts ataraxia, or peacefulness of brain—a term strangely unique about the one favored by the apatheia, Stoics, or absence of aggravating feelings, as might surface beneath.

In a more extended area, II.20, is entitled "Against the Epicureans and the Scholastics," toward the start whereby Epictetus challenges the false front, mentally regarding adversaries' hypotheses, that he comprehends quite plainly unreasonable and in spite of sound judgment: "[1] Even individuals who deny that announcements can be substantial or impressions clear [that is, the Skeptics] are obliged to make utilization of both. You may practically say that nothing demonstrates the legitimacy of an announcement more than discovering somebody compelled to utilize it while in the meantime denying that it is sound." Epictetus does progress to recommend the mix up in Epicurus, since he educates an existence with respect to resigned peacefulness far from society, but then tries to compose books about it, in this manner exposing himself as worry regarding society's welfare all things considered: "[15] What compelled him to get up and compose the things he composed was, obviously, the most grounded component in an individual—nature—which regardless of the resistance made him her subject.

Epictetus spites the conversation essentially, among the Scholastics as he assaults the Skeptics: "What a tragedy! [28] What's going on with you? You substantiate yourself wrong once a day, and still, you won't surrender these seats without moving endeavors. When you partake, where is your hand taken—to your eye or your mouth? What do you venture into when you bathe? At the point when did you ever mix up your pot for a dish, or you're serving spoon for a stick?" He perceives the legitimacy in his condemnation —beyond any doubt in Stoic mold—avoiding hypothetical stands, however more of common sense grounds: "[35] We could give miscreants reason for defending their conduct; such contentions could give appearances to abuse state finances; an insubordinate young fellow could be encouraged further to oppose his folks. So what, as indicated by you, is great or terrible, righteous or awful—either?"

All things being equal, not all Stoics dismisses either Scholarly or Luxurious thoughts out and out. I have said Marcus Aurelius' relative "skepticism" about Fortune versus Iotas (however he unmistakably favored the primary alternative, in accordance with standard Stoic educating), and Seneca is regularly thoughtful to Luxurious perspectives, however, as noted by Gill (2003, note 58), the lightest of the opponent's school of thoughts would be in harmony with Stoic ones, and this is in the soul of its demonstration. He does state plainly, notwithstanding, having Normal Inquiries: "I don't concur with [all] the perspectives of our school" (2014, VII.22.1).

Cicero, in the third Book of De Finibus, gives a few views that differentiate amongst Aristotelians and Stoics, using his fanciful discourse together with the more youthful Cato. At [41] Cicero expresses: "Carneades never stopped to battle that overall purported 'issue of good and malevolence,' there was no contradiction as to actualities between the Stoics and the Peripatetics, however, just as to terms. As far as concerns me, in any case, nothing appears to me more show than that there is to a greater extent a genuine than a verbal distinction of feeling between those savants on these focuses." He proceeds with: "The Peripatetic say that every one of the things which under their framework are called merchandise add to joy; while our school does not trust that aggregate bliss includes everything that should have a specific measure of significant worth joined to it," alluding that treating diversely of the "outer products" amongst Stoics and Aristotelians.

In existence are many archived cases of Stoic conclusions changing in guide reaction that arises from the different schools having obstacles, taking an example of the determinism position that was adjusted and received by Philopator (80-140 C.E.), and a consequence of feedback from the Center Platonist thinkers as well as the Peripatetic. Likewise, there are crystal examples of Stoic thoughts that different schools are joining, like Antiochus, who presented Stoic ideas as he updated Platonism, advocating the change as he asserted that both Aristotle (as well as Zeno, so far as that is concerned) created thoughts verifiable in Plato according to Gill (2003). At long last, Christianity was inclusive of Stoicism using Center Platonism, at any rate from Alexandria's (150-215 C.E.) Lenient.

IV. THE THREE TOPOI

Stoicism is founded on two main topoi, Logic and Physics, but as a result of the Romans choosing to focus on ethics in the Imperial period, they became three topoi of Stoicism, logic, physics, and ethics. Logic, according to the Stoics is the comprehension of the functions of logos or universal reason. Physics, on the other hand, was a topos that focused on metaphysics, theology and natural sciences. Ethics was the more practical topos focusing on the self and morality.

Stoicism as a philosophy is Naturalistic and hence, the first two topoi, logic and physics have a connection with Ethics. Stoics refer to metaphysical entities and beings such as God as physical. To understand the correlation between the topos, we shall look at them combined as a garden. The soil would represent physics; logic would be the fence while the fruits would be the ethics. This is because the physics provides nutrition by way of knowledge, the logic protects the precious within, and the ethics are the actual object in focus of Stoic teachings.

Let us look at each of them.

LOGIC

The Stoics relied on a concept that is based on the process of cognition together with morality due to the connection between logic and physics as well as work in service of the ethics. The Stoics then inferred that not all impressions are true and some were cataleptic (leading to comprehension), and others aren't. The difference is, the cataleptic impression stems from something that exists and agrees with the stamped and engraved things that exist. The non-cataleptic stems from something that either does not exist and if it does, then not in accordance with the existing thing and is unclear and not distinctive.

The Stoics conceive that in a scenario of dreams, an individual's perception qualifies for incorrect but one can be trained to make distinctions between impressions that are cataleptic and those that aren't. However, one should realize that cataleptic impressions cannot be termed as knowledge since knowledge is based on strong impressions that are not altered by reason.

PROPOSITIONAL LOGIC

The Stoics broader approach to logic, however, is characterized as propositional logic which is accredited to one of Zeno's teachers, Diodorus Cronus. It is centered on statements of proposition instead of terms and made essential differences between payables and assertable. This approach to logics made it fundamentally different to Aristotle's logic.

"Define for yourself the thing that is presented to you, so that you know what it is made of, in its nudity, in its completeness, and identify its name, and the elements with which it has been created with. You won't find any product that can scan through everything that comes into your life, and see at the same time, what universe this is, and the use of everything that is in it, and the value of the sum of the parts of the whole." Marcus Aurelius (Meditations)

PHYSICS

Physics, as a Stoic topos would be a natural science as is referred today, metaphysics and theology. The Stoics sought to live in accordance with nature, which therefore means that we need to understand nature. According to Stoics perception, everything is real, everything in existence is corporeal, the universe included which Stoics viewed as material reasoning substance they called nature or God. They adapted to a vitalist comprehension of nature which they divided into two categories: Active and passive. The active one acknowledged both fate and reason, which they called Logos while the passive one, substance, and matter.

"The universe and its soul are God; God is the same principle, operating in reason, with nature and the existence of everything; it is still the essence of the future; fire the principle of life; then the natural elements that transition from one state to the other, like water, air, earth, the sun, moon, stars and the universe at large", Chrysippus, in Cicero (De Natura Deorum)

They believed that everything is subjected to the laws of fate. The universe occurs as it pleases.

"The universe should be taken to be one unit of life, a soul substance; and how everything in the world works in the same energy. All things working together make the world exist as it does; also observe the progressive structure of the web." Marcus Aurelius (Meditations)

ETHICS

As previously mentioned and later expounded on in the next chapter — Roman Stoicism, the Stoics moved to a more practical subject, Ethics, as opposed to the first two topoi that were theoretical. The basis of Stoic Ethics was borrowed from the Cynics. Its key rule was "follow where reason leads." Therefore, it was essential for one to avoid and be free of any passion. Passion was their traditional meaning for suffering. This was sought to be achieved through peace of mind, which was a state of having a clear judgment. Plato taught four principal virtues: Courage, temperance, wisdom, and justice.

CHAPTER TWO

GREEK STOICISM

The "Greek" period that belonged to Stoa covers both the first and second durations, starting from the school established by Zeno to the change in gravity's focal point from Athens to Rome in the First Century B.C.E. during the Posidonius season, who turned into Cicero's companion —who wasn't a Stoic, but rather among the best circuitous early Stoicism sources. The conception of stoicism is not recent, despite the prosperity in Athens, despite the fact that the vast majority of its types started from the Eastern Mediterranean: Citium leading to Zeno (present day Cyprus), Assos leading to Cleanthes (current Western Turkey), and Soli leading to Chrysippus (current Southern Turkey), to mention just a few. As per Mixture (2003), the particular example is essentially an impression of the predominant social flow during that time, as per the influence of the successes of Alexander.

Originating from the earliest starting point, Stoicism is and was solidly a "Socratic" theory, with the Stoics not fretting such a mark. Zeno's examinations began under the Critic Boxes by himself, and Pessimism dependably impacted Stoicism, the distance to the later works of Epictetus. In any case, Zeno additionally considered as a part of his instructors Polemo, the Foundation's leader, and Stilpo, from the Megarian school established by Euclid of Megara, a student of Socrates. Zeno's significance surfaced when he expounded a reasoning that was both of clear Socratic motivation (ideals that are Main Great) as well as a bargain amongst both Stilpo's and Polemo's positions, as initially supported there are outer products—however, they are of auxiliary significance—while the second one guaranteed that nothing outside could be great or awful. That trade off comprised in the exceptionally Stoic idea that outside merchandise is of morally impartial esteem, however, are regardless of the protest of regular interest.

Zeno set up the tripartite investigation of Stoic reasoning (see the three topoi involving morals, material science, and rationale). The morals were fundamentally a direct form of Criticism; the material science was affected according to Taran (1971) by Plato's Timaeus as well as enveloped a universe penetrated by a dynamic (referred to as, sound) plus a latent rule, and also a grandiose labyrinth of circumstances as well as results; through which rationale included both what today is alluded to as epistemology and formal rationale, further explained as an informational hypothesis, which according to Stoics was firmly empiricist-naturalistic.

Stoics from earlier could likewise be willfully hostile to exact in their rational theology from works by Zeno, taking a scenario of Chrysippus belief that protecting one's heart, not one's mind, is the seat of insight. This conflicted with entirely definitive anatomical confirmation that was at that point accessible in the Greek time frame and Galen's hatred stemmed from this (such as Tieleman, 2002). Stoics updated their conviction on the issue later on.

Despite the tactless act that occurred previously, Chrysippus was the aggressively persuasive Stoic mastermind, who was in charge of the school's upgrade, which declined under the direction of Cleanthes. The upgrade included an expansive systemization of its lessons. The presentation of several novel ideas rationally is one of Stoicism segment's that had the most specialized philosophical effect for a long period of time. A composition by Diogenes Laertius (2015, VII.183) stated that "Yet for Chrysippus, there had been no Yard."

There were only two leaders of the Stoa after Chrysippus, from Babylon, Diogenes and from Bone-structure (which was south-focal Turkey) was Zeno. Their commitments were far less noteworthy than those done by Chrysippus. Until 155 B.C.E, there had been no significant event that took place. The leaders of the three important schools in Athens; the Peripatetic, the Scholastics and the Stoics; were all sent to Rome and the end goal is to help with political endeavors.

The fourth school, the Luxurious one, was missing, because of its non-contribution in political issues. This is important to note, as Sedley (2003) also noted this. A colossal connection was established on the Roman open, by Stoics Diogenes of Babylon and other thinkers with their open exhibitions (this evidently, a similarly troubling one on the Roman tip top, in this way starting a long convention of pressure amongst logicians and abnormal state government officials that portrayed particularly the post-Republican domain), clearing the street, which was a move done later so as to reason with Rome from Athens. In addition, there were different focuses of learning, similar to Alexandria.

Starting with Antipater of Bone structure, and after that all the more Panaetius and Posidonius, the Stoics returned to their association with the Foundation, particularly the significance of Stoic cosmology, Timaeus, as previously mentioned. Posidonius was greatly intrigued by the way Pluto's principle character, during the discourse, is a Pythagorean. This was a school that according to Posidonius, to some level, misguidedly figured out how to connect to Stoicism.

It gives the idea that the more extensive venture sought after by both Panaetius and Posidonius was one of looking for shared belief (according to Sedley 2003 in the utilizations of the expression "syncretism") that was among the Academicism, Aristotelianism, and Stoicism. These three are considered the branches of Socratic reasoning.

Once the logicians of the different schools moved to Rome from Athens, after the 88-86 B.C.E diaspora, the procedure would have provided a limited extent in charge of the further achievement of Stoicism.

CHAPTER THREE

STOICISM IN ROME

In 155 B.C.E, the visit by the head of various philosophical schools in Rome was seen as a significant event because it led to the introduction of rationality to the consideration of the Romans. Yet, in 88-86 B.C.E, the political occasions that occurred brought a huge change in the Western theory when all is said and done, and Stoicism specifically, for the rest of olden times.

During that era, scholars, especially the Peripatetic Athenian and—shockingly—the Luxurious Aristion, who were in control in Athens did make the mistake of agreeing to go against the Romans with the Mithridates (Bugh 1992). The Ruler of Pontus and also that of Athens was an issue, especially to Athens. It led to the diaspora of logicians all over the Mediterranean.

There is no real evidence that shows the school of Stoa did continue in Athens after Panaetius, who kept himself away and went to Rome, it has come to the conclusion that Posidonius did not instruct in Athens but in Rome.

Be that as it may, as per Sedley 2003, the lasting effects of the events that took place in 88-86 B.C.E shifted the focal point of Stoicism gravity to Rome from Greek support. In Rhodes, there was a prospering Luxurious school and Bone structure. Stoic was once picked by Augustus to be a guide in representing the city. Critically, in any case, Stoicism ended up noticeably vital, inspiring the move between the Realm, and the late Republic together with the Cato.

In the long run, turning into a good example for later Stoics as a result of his political confinement to the "tyrant" Julius Caesar. Sedley highlights two stoic intellectuals of the late First Century B.C.E, Athenodorus of Bone structure and Arius Didymus, as a trailblazer of one of the best and most debatable Stoic figures, Seneca.

Both Athenodorus and Arius were near and dear teachers to the chief ruler, Augustus, and Arius even made a letter out of consolation to Livia, on Augustus' better half, pertaining to the passing of her child, which Seneca later hailed as a sort of point of view work of enthusiastic treatment, the sort of work he was possessed with and ended up plainly renowned for.

When we get to the Supreme period (Gill 2003), we see a choice to move far from the more hypothetical parts of Stoicism (the "material science" and "rationale," see underneath) and toward more down to earth medications of the morals. In any case, as Gill brings up, this ought not to lead us to feel that the vitality of Stoicism had taken a crash by then: we know about new different treatises conveyed by Stoic writers of that period, on everything running from ethics (Hierocles' Components of Morals) to material science (Seneca's Normal Inquiries), and the Rundown of the Customs of Greek Religious logic by Cornutus as one of an unobtrusive pack of complete Stoic treatises to get from the authentic background of the school.

Regardless, it is verifiably the case that the best known Stoics of the time were either educators like Musonius Rufus and Epictetus or the politically powerful, like Seneca and Marcus Aurelius, thus framing our understanding of the period as unpredictable to the foundational and more theoretical one of Zeno and Chrysippus.

Imperatively, it is from the late Republic and Domain that we moreover get a part of the best-underhanded sources on Stoicism, particularly, a couple of books by Cicero. (Furthermore, this writing went ahead to impact later essayists well after the root of Stoicism, particularly Plotinus (205-270 C.E.) and even the 6th Century C.E. Neoplatonist Simplicius.

Most of the above regardless, what is most vital about Stoicism in the midst of the Roman Majestic period, in any case, is in like manner what clearly had the theory's effect resonate consistently, in the long run prompting two recoveries, the alleged Neostoicism of the Renaissance, and the present "current Stoicism" improvement to which I will move in the direction of the completion of this paper. The wellsprings of such centrality were on a very basic level two: from one perspective, alluring instructors like Musonius and Epictetus, and then again Seneca and Marcus were the persuasive political figures

Musonius was, it could be said, both: It was not just that he was an individual from the Roman "knight" class, and the educator of Epictetus, he was also politically powerful, straightforwardly denouncing the courses of action of both Nero and Vespasian, and getting expelled twice appropriately.

Seneca was not just more open to the quest for "favored indifferent" (he was an affluent Representative, however, it appears to be unreasonable to blame him for supporting a short sighted, self-serving objectivity: see the nuanced histories by Romm 2014 and Wilson 2014), yet unequivocally communicated that he was denouncing of a segment of the standards of the early Stoics, and that he was keen on picking up from various schools, including the Epicureans. Comprehensively, Marcus Aurelius was open—one would for all intents and purposes need to state realist—about logic, at a couple of centers in the Contemplations (1997) unequivocally communicating the two choices of "Fortune" (Stoic instructing) or "Particles" (the Luxurious take), for example: "Either there is a deadly need and invulnerable request, or a kind Provision, or a disarray without a reason and an executive. On the off chance that at that point there is a powerful need, why do you stand up to? In any case, if there is a Fortune that enables itself to be appeased, make yourself deserving of the assistance of the eternality. However, in the event that there is a perplexity without a senator, be content that in such a whirlwind you have yourself a specific decision insight" (XII.14); or: "regarding what may transpire from without, consider that it happens either by shot or as indicated by Provision, and you should neither accuse chance nor denounce Fortune" (XII.24).

Stoicism was perfectly healthy amid the Roman time frame, despite the fact that the accentuation shifted—to some degree normally, one may include—from setting out the central thoughts to making them better and also training them in the social and individual life.

CHAPTER FOUR

NEUROPLASTICITY

Neuroplasticity is a general term that identifies with the brain's ability to change itself, functionally and physically, in a life of a person; because of the environment, thinking, emotions and behavior. Neuroplasticity has been known for quite a while. The possibility of a changing cerebrum has supplanted the once held conviction that the grown-up mind was a static organ physiologically or that it was hard-wired after periods in our youth that formatted it.

PRINCIPLES OF NEUROPLASTICITY

The book *Soft-Wired*, by Dr. McKay's, explains how the Brain Plasticity in New Science can revolutionize someone's brain, Dr. Merzenich lists few principles that can remodel your brain:

1. Change is constrained to those circumstances in which the brain is in the state of mind for it. If you are ready, on the

ball, connected with, roused, good to go, the cerebrum discharges the neurochemicals important to empower mind change.

2. What changes in the cerebrum are the characteristics of the relationship of neurons that are secured together, step by step, in time. The more something is sharpened; the more affiliations are changed and made to fuse all segments of the experience (tangible information, development, psychological examples). You can consider it like an "ace controller" being molded for that particular direction, which empowers it to be performed with striking office and reliability after some time.

3. Learning-driven changes in affiliations increase cell-to-cell coordinated effort, which is basic for growing resolute quality. Merzenich elucidates this by requesting you to imagine the sound from a football stadium stacked with fans all praising erratically versus similar individuals applauding as one. He clarifies, "The more capably organized your [nerve cell] groups are, the more capable and more dependable their behavioral preparations."

4. Associations between groups of neurons and the brain are fortified such that they speak to isolate snapshots of progressive things that dependably happen in serial time. This empowers your brain to anticipate what happens next and have a diligent "familiar stream." Without this limit,

your nonstop stream would be diminished to "a movement of discrete, stagnating puddles," illuminates Merzenich.

5. The beginning of changes are brief. Your cerebrum at first records the change, by then chooses in the event that it should reveal the change never-ending or not. It just winds up doubtlessly interminable if your mind judges the experience to be enamoring or adequately novel or if the behavioral outcome is basic, awesome or horrendous.

6. The psyche is changed by internal mental practice in comparable ways and including precisely comparative techniques that control changes fulfilled through joint efforts with the external world. As demonstrated by Merzenich, "You don't have to move an inch to drive positive plastic change in your mind. You're inside depictions of things investigated from memory work suitable for dynamic personality malleability based learning."

7. Memory helpers and controls learning. As you take in another expertise, your cerebrum observes and recalls the great endeavors, while disposing of the not all that great try. At that point, it reviews the last great pass, makes incremental modifications, and dynamically progresses.

8. Each development of learning gives a snapshot of chance to the mind to balance out — and lessen the problematic energy of — possibly meddling foundations or "noise." Each time your cerebrum reinforces an association by propelling

your dominance of ability, it additionally debilitates different relationship of neurons that weren't used at that correct moment. This negative plastic personality change annihilates a part of the irrelevant or intruding activity in the cerebrum.

CHAPTER FIVE

UNDERSTANDING EMOTIONS

Stoics always feel. This is not one of enthusiastic restraint. Despite what might be expected, it is an expectation of Stoics that quietness and euphoria are brought about by living your life to the fullest. All things considered, individuals appear to liken Stoics, to Vulcan wannabes. Nothing against Vulcans besides their paternalistic approach towards humankind in the pre-Federation years but there are bad stoic good examples like additional terrestrials. Stoics are understudies of being human.

The stoic maxim, live as indicated by nature, moves us to figure out where in this growing universe we fit in. Everything that is chaotic and totally bizarre in this world that connects life is included here. Doubtlessly, we concentrate the greater part of what is our consideration on human personality, which on its own is an astounding instrument. The mental scene is made up of feelings and this is where Stoics do give it their due. There is always that nagging thought of not fully commending them on their discovery.

In this passionate life, quite different from how we deal with it, Stoics have their own way of dealing with it. For example, we don't anticipate that feelings will be great aids for conduct. Climate can be a way to say how these feelings are treated like. You are required to drive slowly, carry an umbrella when there is rain, yet you need to work in the end. Passionate tempests are quite similar in a way. Despite having a terrible feeling towards some things, Stoics believe we can still act well at present.

If you're to a great degree inconsiderate to your associates and, when inquired as to why, you replied, "it's sticky," individuals would perceive you as amusing. Stoics would state that snapping at individuals since you're furious is similarly unreasonable. In the first place, your outrage itself is most likely because of receiving an unhelpful point of view. Second, regardless, a man has the option of acting with uprightness regardless of the situations.

There are three "positive sentiments" that Stoicism run by. In Greek, they are referred to as hai apatheia. These sentiments are Caution, Wish, and Joy. There are three Passions that are considered "awful sentiments" of Stoic reasoning. The distinction was created to separate the positive from the negative sentiments. In psyche, the Stoic lineup is...

Joy v. Pleasure

Wish v. Appetite (Lust)

Caution v. Fear

I wouldn't contend on the off chance that to you the rundown does look rather odd. It requires a background knowledge on this subject to see how people of old reached these conclusions, and, after it's all said and done, you may think they're nuts. Look at this article on Stoic morals on the off chance that you need a taste. As far as it matters for me, I need to bring up that Joy, Pleasure, and so forth are all-encompassing classifications.

Every one of the subtleties of human feeling can be categorized with one of these words, so don't stress over begrudge, covetousness, seethe, vindictiveness, etc..., they're altogether represented. Gracious and the fourth energy, Distress. Pain cannot be an inverse and Misery is troubling.

Next is Wish. It is a peculiar name for an enthusiastic idea. Why you might wonder, do Stoics consider Appetite awful and Wish great? It might be due to the fact that, according to the Marcus Aurelius citation I began with, take into consideration that this movement is entirely feasible for you to do. Stoics pin for things that you don't require or see as the tremendous misuse of vitality.

The definition of the energy Appetite according to us is, "the silly yearning or quest for a normal descent." Greed is a hunger for tangible/material things; whereas Hostility is the quest for vindicating. Our vitality is consumed by these things on a dream, or as they tend to do, make us perform useless activities. Things that are out of control are things that Stoics do not wager their joy on. They'd rather wish than accept Appetite.

According to Aurelius, you have to delight in your activity. When Stoics discuss feeling, it is always to influence; the cognizant, subjective part of a feeling that is considered separate from the real changes.

Hunger isn't about seeing a man who is per your standards, it is that inclination in addition to the prospect that keeps running with it, says "Dammann NN," and afterward lines it all with a mental symbolism. The mental segment, according to Stoicism, is a decision, one that is undesirable. There can be a superior effect that can be asserted; Wish that is fulfilling and enduring too.

When you delight in an activity, it is always possible for you to get through it.

Wish is not known, but its influence states that it says "I should have x. However my satisfaction is not situated in x." In context, it is a move. The things that are to make you happy are Hunger. Wish on the other hand says that there are other fabulous things in the world, but I will not find my happiness in them. The first standard of Stoic is that having a wish like behavior is the main thing that is under our control and righteousness is the main great. It is conceivable to be content; this is according to Stoics point of view. It is not an easy feat, as there is no guarantee that going along with this is simple. Instead of Appetite, Wish is an influence that provides a true and rich ground to have insightful activities.

A comparative rationale is that of Caution versus Pleasure versus Fear. Fear is neglecting a normal threat and it makes us throw away the satisfaction we have at present because we think that something or someone will come and take it away from us. Caution is more of knowing that curveballs are going to be coming our way and it is up to us to be arranged at the same time, by and by, genuine peace isn't found in outer things. On the off chance that we will prosper, we should approach the world not with caution but with mindfulness.

Pleasure, according to the negative perspective of Stoics, is additional because of Joy's outer core interest. Stoic's try to build up a withstanding Joy, setup of momentary snapshots of pleasure. By and by, I don't attempt to debilitate the feelings of excitement that I have. I attempt to remember what makes me feel excited by need, be transient and it is quite conceivable to exist without such things.

As we said before, Stoics feel. "Walking it off" is not a rationale that we conclude on. We require and insist on the best for individuals, this is because of the standard low points and high points in our lives. We think that most of the agony we go through is self-delivered, this is as a result of a perspective that requires we see the world not as it is or in a similar way. Fragile, mortal things, expectation-past expectations- are the interests that we concentrate on the most such that they keep on. What is distinctive is Caution, Happiness, and Wish. This comes from a mind that acknowledges changes do happen; meaning that what is in us can thrive and survive.

CHAPTER SIX

STOICISM AND FREE WILL

The traditional Stoics were compatibilists, having confidence in total determinism and furthermore through and through freedom, and attesting straightforwardly that the two don't conflict. They stated that there are no occasions that don't take after definitely from causes. They even don't have an issue with the "start" of the universe, since they trusted it to be cyclic, expanding endlessly into the past and future.

On the off chance that one characterizes "free will" as the presence of uncaused occasions, at that point no, they didn't have confidence in through and through freedom, however, they stated that such uncaused occasions were not required for moral obligation, opportunity, or the greater part of the standard things individuals connect with choice.

Chrysippus, the pioneer of the Stoic rationality, characterized destiny, which the Greeks call εἱμαρμένη, in about the accompanying terms: "Destiny," he says, "is an interminable and unalterable arrangement of conditions, and a chain rolling and snaring itself through an unbroken arrangement of outcomes, from which it is molded and made up."

But I have duplicated Chrysippus' exceptional words, as precisely as I could review them, all together that, if my elucidation ought to appear to be excessively dark, making it impossible for anybody, he may turn his thoughtfulness regarding the thinker's particular dialect. For in the fourth book of his work On Providence, he says that εἱμαρμένη is "an efficient arrangement, built up by nature, of all occasions, tailing each other and consolidated from time everlasting, and their unalterable Association."

In any case, the creators of different perspectives and of different schools of logic transparently scrutinize this definition as it takes after: "If Chrysippus," they say, "trusts that everything is gotten under way and coordinated by destiny, and that the course of destiny and its curls can't be turned aside or avoided, at that point the transgressions and issues of men too should not cause outrage or be ascribed to themselves and their slants, however to a specific unavoidable drive which emerges from destiny."

This is the courtesan and mediator for goodness' sake, and by which whatever is to happen shall happen; and that along with these lines the building up of punishments for the blameworthy by law is unjustifiable, if men don't deliberately carry out violations, yet are driven into them by destiny.

Against these reactions, Chrysippus finally contends the nuance astutely, however the indication of all that he has composed regarding that matter is about this: "In spite of the fact that it is a reality," he says, "that everything is liable to an unavoidable and major law and are firmly connected to destiny, yet the unconventional properties of our psyches are liable to destiny just as per their uniqueness and quality.

For if in the first place they are molded by nature for well-being and value, they will stay away with little resistance and little trouble all that drive with which destiny debilitates them from without. If by any chance, they are unpleasant, oblivious, rough, and with no help from training, through their own perversity and deliberate drive they dive into persistent blames and sin, despite the fact that the strike of some burden because of destiny be slight or non-existent. Also, this very thing ought to occur along these lines because of that common and unavoidable association of occasions which is called "destiny." For it is in the idea of things, as it were, destined and inescapable that shrewd characters ought not to be free from sins and blames."

A little later he utilizes a delineation of this announcement of his, which is in truth very perfect and proper: "For example," he said, "in the event that you roll around and hollow stone over a slanting, soaked bit of ground, you do for sure outfit the start and reason for its quick plummet, yet soon its moves forward, not on account of you making it do as such, but rather in view of its curious frame and regular propensity to roll; just so the request, the law, and the unavoidable nature of destiny gotten under way the different classes of things and the beginnings of causes, yet the doing of our plans and considerations, and even our activities, are controlled by every individual's own particular will and the attributes of his psyche."

In the setting both of exchanges on compatibilism and of "what is in our control", the critical piece of Stoic terminology eph' hêmin (ἐφ' ἡμῖν), typically made an interpretation of as "up to us, what is in our energy", is truly better interpretation as "inferable from us", an outcome of our character. Eph' hêmin is utilized as a part of dialogs of through and through freedom and furthermore in various places in Epictetus, for example, the primary sentence of the Enchiridion.

Stoic physics recognized "principle" from "auxiliary" causes. If by any chance there is a chain of causation, A causes B causes C causes D, at that point, everything is the principal cause for the following in the chain, while everything preceding it is a helper cause. In this way, A will be an auxiliary cause for C, yet just B is the principal cause. In like manner, B is just a helper reason for D, and just C is the standard reason. (Cicero, On Fate book.)

For A to be the principal cause of B, at that point An unquestionable requirement comes into coordinate physical contact with B. Keep in mind, the Stoics trusted that lone "bodies" exist, and respect things like personality, and so on as physical bodies, much like a current realist sees the cerebrum. The most obvious approach to refresh Stoic science in such manner is say that the explanatory personality is a body covering those parts of the mind in charge of cognizant, logical idea. Eph' hêmin alludes particularly to those things of which the explanatory personality is the rule cause. Stoics believed that the main critical thing for destiny or pure determination is that everything is associated with secondary causes, while the main essential thing with the expectation of complimentary will, is that the psyche is the ruling reason for a few things. Hence, there is no logical inconsistency.

CHAPTER SEVEN

STOICISM AND MODERN LIFE

Stoicism is etched in being indifferent to pleasure, joy, pain, and grief. In modern life, it may refer to repression of feelings and patiently endure. Despite Stoicism being virtually associated with being emotionless, it can be used and channeled towards living a satisfactory life. Regardless of the fact that it is an old philosophy, it can, has, and is being practiced in modern and contemporary life as we know it. Fundamentally, it entails minimizing and reducing negative emotions in one's life and putting focus on joy and gratitude, heedful practices and living according to values.

Let us look at 5 principles that are derivatives of Stoicism towards Modern living.

1. Do not focus on events you cannot control, instead, give your attitude a do-over.

"You have power over your mind – not outside events. Realize this, and you will find strength."

– Marcus Aurelius (Meditations)

Identify the events in your life that are circumstantial and are beyond your human ability to change or control them and let them be. It would be pointless to get frustrated over them and waste time and energy trying to change them. Instead, change your attitude and perception. Through this realization, we cannot be influenced by external event, we can also in turn control our reactions, and our minds become impenetrable.

2. Imagine life without possessions and people and justly appreciate them.

"Do not indulge in dreams of having what you have not, but reckon up the chief of the good things in one's life, and thankfully remember how you would crave for them if they were not yours."

– Marcus Aurelius (Meditations)

The more one wants, the more dissatisfied they are. This begs the question then of how one finds happiness. Gratitude. We, therefore, have to be grateful for what we have and find joy in it. This is derived from a Stoic practice of imagining you lost some important possessions. The outcome would be that one learns to appreciate them rather than seeking others. In case, one loses something or they are always taken; one should be grateful that they had the object, even if just over a period rather than being upset that they lost it. The Stoics taught that we borrow everything from the universe and by being grateful, goodness remains in our lives and joy manifests from that despite things coming and going.

3. Don't just preach your values, live by them.

"Don't explain your philosophy. Embody it."   – Epictetus

Stoicism is deeply embedded in personal values. One should understand that every decision they make contains certain moral implications. One should constantly ask themselves how they should behave in every situation and make choices and decision based on personal values. In short, everyone should have a moral code and live by it.

4. Do not abide by the materialistic nature of the society

"Wealth is not wanting the materialistic, but in having few wants."   – Epictetus

This principle is short and precise; if we endeavor to want less, there is a decrease in desire, and we eventually are satisfied more by what we have.

5. In your dealings be cheerful.

"A man thus grounded must, by his will or not, necessarily be attended by constant cheerfulness and joy that is deep and issues from deep within, since he finds delight in his resources, and desires no joys greater than his inner joys." – Seneca

One should enjoy all things of life, even the simple ones and learn that they cannot control every situation, therefore, be truly cheerful in all interactions

In summary, do not get caught up in materialism, be cheerful always, work diligently and know what you can and cannot control as this is the Stoic way.

HOW TO BE CALM

As previously covered, Stoics sought to act on their principles and virtues and not passions/emotions. We observed in previous chapters about the three principles of Stoicism, Epictetus, Marcus Aurelius and Seneca who all faced adversities but chose to remain calm regardless.

At about A.D. 55 in Hierapolis, Phrygia, Epictetus was conceived a slave on the Eastwards outskirts of the Roman Empire. Right off the bat, he was enthusiastic about his rationality, and with the approval of his proprietor, he always fancied the Stoic reasoning under the guidance of, Gaius Musonius Rufus. Right after the passing of Nero, who was the fifth Roman ruler, who ruled with oppression and brutality, Epictetus showed his reasoning in Rome. He, later on, advanced to Greece where he started to teach his philosophy through a school that majored on Stoicism. His school was well known and he taught, Marcus Aurelius, who was soon to become the Emperor of Greece.

In A.D. 121, Marcus Aurelius was born, a ruler who has been termed as the best Roman emperor who ever lived. He is famously known for his habit of writing the undertakings and lessons in his diary. His diary is what soon became the valuable book, Meditations. It is the book that has filled in as updates for Stoic rule that concentrated on modesty, mindfulness, benefit, passing, nature, and that's only the tip of the iceberg.

One other renowned Roman Stoic thinker is Seneca. Seneca was a mentor, an established statesman, and guide to Nero. He is famously known for the works which include many expositions and 124 letters that include subjects like training, fellowship, common obligation, moral commitment, quietude, mindfulness, discipline, and that's just the beginning. Some of his admirers include Emerson, Montaigne, John Stuart Mill and Tom Wolfe.

We are going to look at some of my most loved standards from the Stoic classes of logic, the majority of them relate to the three scholars. If grasped and practiced frequently, the fundamentals of Stoicism will spearhead your innovativeness, encourage the work process you undertake, and enhance the general perspective of your life. Innovative work expects us to be helpless, dedicated, versatile, and gallant, and all these require an outlook which refutes diversions or negative driving forces while concentrating on what is essential. It's an intense exercise in careful control.

Without a rationality to direct our work and life, we will determinedly surrender to our reasons and diversions. We will commit the agreeable error of following up on our mindsets and not on our standards.

1. Remember that failure is not the end.
"Does what's happened, keep you from being generous, practicing self-control, sanity, honesty, prudence, humility, straightforwardness, and all other qualities that allow self-fulfillment? So, remember this principle when you are vulnerable to pain: the thing itself was no misfortune at all; to endure it and come out victorious is great fortune."

— Marcus Aurelius, Meditations

Without failure, there is no growth. One must realize that there is life after failure and let it not offset their emotions.

2. It is important to know that emotions are developed and experienced from the inside of you.
"Today I escaped anxiety. Or no, I discarded it, because it was within me, in my perceptions — not outside."

— Meditations of Marcus Aurelius.

External events cannot affect our emotions, rather, it is what we tell ourselves that provokes feelings on it. Before reacting to situations, look within and not what is around you.

3. Identify someone you can trust and be honest with them.
Choose someone whose way of life reflects what comes out of the mouth, and someone who mirrors the character of the person who owns that face, reserve your judgment. Always point out this individual to yourself and see the person as either your model or your guardian. This is what I call a MUST perspective in someone's life, whereby the characters are the measures we are looking at. If there is no ruler to work on, it will not make things straight against you."

— Seneca, Letters From a Stoic

Similar to failure, find people you deem role models and can connect with on a personal level. Use these people to relay and communicate whenever you feel the urge, to be honest, and need advice.

4. Remember that the greatest resource you have is time.
"Not to live as if you had endless years ahead of you. Death overshadows you. While you're alive and able - be generous."

— Marcus Aurelius

Stoicism is such an interesting philosophy, and what I love and is by far hard to follow is that passing is at the cutting edge of their considerations. Stoics understood that people are vaporous ideas and it is rehashed in numerous aspects of life.

This produces a dire feeling, to understand that you have within you a specific amount of time in your hands, but you are not sure about the specified time that is assured, as the ones you have already lived. When these thoughts come to mind, I understand that regular is a chance to enhance, not in the direction of banality; but rather to genuinely figure out what we acknowledge as fit for accomplishing and how we are extremely in charge of the nature of our lives.

5. Remind yourself not to procrastinate.
"At dawn, when you have trouble sleeping, tell yourself: 'I have to go to work—as a human being. Why do I need to worry if I will just do what I was born to do? The things I am meant to accomplish in this world? Might this be my purpose? To hide under the blankets?

—But it's nicer here…

So were you born to feel 'nice' instead of doings things and experiencing them? Don't you see the plants, the ants, the birds, bees and spiders going about their tasks, putting the world in order, and you're not willing to do your job as a human being? Why aren't you running to do what you are meant to do?

—But we have to sleep sometime…

Agreed. But nature set a limit on that—as it did on relishing food and drinks. And you're over the limit. You've had more than enough of that. But not of working. There you're still below your quota. You don't love yourself enough. Or you'd love your nature too. People who love what they do give their own while engaging in it, they even forget to wash or eat. Don't you respect yourself more than the engraver does for engraving, the dancer for dance, the miser for the social climber for status or the money? When they're possessed by what they do, they'd rather stop eating and sleeping than give up practicing their arts." — Meditations by Marcus Aurelius.

In the instance one is unable to focus or work on necessary tasks, the above text can go a long way to provide great motivation.

6. Read with resolution and apply your learnings.
"Don't just say you have read books. Show that through them you have learned to be a reflective thinker. Knowledge seeking is the training weights of the mind. It is not proper to assume that one has made progress simply by having internalized their contents."

— The Art of Living by Epictetus.

Reading readies your brain, even encourages you to maintain a strategic distance from silly errors, yet toward the finish of everything, there must be the aftereffect of some activity:

disappointment, perhaps a win, or a lesson. Education's purpose is to disguise information, in any case, start an activity and encourage more shrewd choices. Perusing self-improvement guides will, at that time, make you feel roused for a change

7. Analyze what you spend most of your on.

"Concentrate on: The value of attentiveness varies in proportion to its object. You're better off not giving very little time to the small things." — Marcus Aurelius, Meditations

As the above quotes suggest, we humans spend a lot of time on negligible things rather than those that matter. We should find out what matters and allocate most our time to it.

8. Challenge yourself to be very honest.

For a person who is oblivious to his wrong actions, does not expect to be corrected. Before you change, you have to catch yourself doing it. There are people who take pride in their failures: imagine someone who is proud of his failures and actually counts them and does not consider salvaging them? Therefore, show that you are guilty in some way, analyze yourself looking at all the evidence that stack against you. First, you need to be the prosecutor, then the judge and later on the pleader of the mitigation. You will need to be strict and harsh to yourself." — Letters From a Stoic by Seneca,

Changing habits is a difficult task. It's essential to be aware of the urges that block us from appearing, connecting with, conferring, and being available. When resistance sets in, use that as a go ahead signal. The test is meant to prepare you to find the best way. This, definitely is not about an ability or some oblivious reflex. The act of mindfulness—to consider your reasoning— by the way you think, feel, and carry on is a muscle.

9. Withdraw from your phone and spend more time focused on the present times

"Nothing, to my way of thinking, is a better evidence of a well-mannered mind than a man's ability to stop just at himself and spend time in his own company."

— Letters From a Stoic by Seneca.

It isn't so much that we live in a time of distractions, but instead, an age where we are neglecting to educate and grasp careful thought processes. To me, a youngster in an eatery, playing a game on her iPad, is the same as a grown-up brushing through Instagram when you have companions with you. The two situations are snapshots of association (to the general population who you interact with, not through your screen), correspondence, and satisfaction. To be available and also figuring out how to be distant from everyone else is a propensity. A few people are decent at it since they set aside a few minutes to do it—truth be told, they require it or else they would go distraught.

EVERYTHING IS UNDER YOUR CONTROL AND MAKING THE BEST OF SITUATIONS

1. Change What You Can — Forget the Rest. The absolute most critical practice in Stoic logic is separating between what we can change and what we can't. What we have impact over and what we don't. As Epictetus expressed, "The central errand in life is just this: to distinguish and isolate matters so I can state plainly to myself which are facades not under my control, and which need to do with the decisions I control."

2. Begin Living — This is one of Seneca's most noteworthy jests: "You fear to bite the dust. Be that as it may, come now, how is this life of yours anything besides passing?" Our dread of biting the dust frequently makes one wonder: To ensure what precisely? For many individuals the appropriate responses are; hours of TV, tattling, glutting, squandering potentials, and answering to an exhausting employment, without any end in sight and on. Today, begin living!

3. Know When to Stick (And When to Quit!) — "Think about the individuals who, not by blame of irregularity but rather by the absence of exertion, are excessively shaky, making it impossible to live as they wish, however just live as they have started." Seneca

4. Respite and Be Grateful — Think of the considerable number of things you can be thankful for now. That you are alive, that you live in a period principally of peace, that you have enough well-being, relaxation, and access to a web association by reading this article. As Seneca kept in touch with his companion Lucilius, "In all things, we should attempt to make ourselves be as appreciative as we could have expected under the circumstances."

5. Keep in mind That You Can't Be Broken — Someone can toss you in chains, yet they don't have the ability to change your identity. Indeed, even under the most noticeably awful torment and brutalities that people can perpetrate on each other, our control over our brain and our energy to settle on our own choices can't be broken. As Epictetus has stated, "You can tie up my leg. However, not even Zeus can break my flexibility of decision."

6. Continuously Love — Here's Seneca citing another Stoic: "Hecato says, 'I can show you an adoration mixture made with no medications, herbs, or uncommon spell—on the off chance that you would be cherished, love.'" The Beatles put it truly well a couple of hundreds of years after the fact, "At last, the affection you take is equivalent to the adoration you make." Not simply in governmental issues, not simply in resistance, but rather in our own lives. There is no circumstance in which contempt makes a difference. However, practically every circumstance is improved by affection.

7. Try not to Burn The Candle On Both Ends — Seneca wrote in his paper On Tranquility of Mind that "the mind must take some time off to relax; it will feel more energized and keen after a decent break." The brain is a muscle, and like the rest, it can be stressed, exhausted, even harmed. Our physical well-being is likewise exhausted by over-commitment, an absence of rest, and unfortunate propensities. Keep in mind: Life is a whole deal. Is it true that you will have the capacity to deal with the troublesome minutes if you've taken on too much work?

8. Burrow Deep Within Yourself — "Burrow profound inside yourself, for there is a wellspring of goodness ever prepared to stream if you will continue burrowing." Marcus Aurelius

9. Be Kind — Most discourteousness, unpleasantness, and mercilessness is a cover for profound situated shortcoming. Generosity in these circumstances is feasible for individuals of extraordinary quality. You have that quality. Utilize it. As Marcus Aurelius put it, "For what can a vengeful person do on the off chance that you continue demonstrating generosity and if given the shot, you delicately bring up where they turned out badly—perfectly fine is attempting to hurt you?"

10. See The Bigger Picture — The Emperor Marcus Aurelius kept in touch with himself to "think about the entire universe of issue and how little you offer." The earth, the extent that science lets us know, is approximately 4.5 billion years of age and hints at no closure soon. Our time on the earth, then again, will be what? Quite a few years, possibly? Consider this whenever you feel vainglorious, or like everything rises and falls on what you do next. It doesn't. You're only one individual among many, doing your best among numerous.

11. Turn out to be Good Now — "Don't carry on as though you are bound to live until the end of time. What's destined hangs over you. For whatever length of time that you live and keeping in mind that you can, turn out to be great at this point." Marcus Aurelius

12. Concentrate Inward—Don't Judge Others — "Let reasoning scratch off your deficiencies, instead of being an approach to rail against the issues of others," composed Seneca. The correct heading of the theory is centered internal—to improve ourselves and to leave other individuals to that undertaking for themselves and their particular trip. Leave other individuals to their flaws.

13. You Choose The Outcome — Epictetus once said that: "He was sent to jail. In any case, the perception 'he has endured detestable,' is an expansion originating from you." An occasion itself is objective. How we portray it—that it was out of line, or it's an extraordinary catastrophe, or that they did it intentionally—is on us.

14. Be A Force For Good — Don't be a malicious person. You should likewise be a drive for good on the planet, decently well. As Marcus Aurelius stated, "Regularly bad form lies in what you aren't doing, not just in what you are doing."

15. Love Your Fate — "Don't look for everything to occur as you wish it would, but instead wish that everything occurs as it really will—at that point your life will stream well, " Epictetus said. Rather than just tolerating what happens, the Stoics ask us to appreciate what has happened—whatever it is. Nietzsche, numerous hundreds of years after the fact, instituted the ideal articulation to catch this thought: love fate (an affection for destiny). It's not recently tolerating; it adores everything that happens.

16. Watch Your Words — "Better to trip with the feet than with the tongue," Zeno composed. You can simply get up after you fall, however, recollect, what has been said can never be inferred. Particularly barbarous and harmful things.

17. Roll out An Inward Improvement — Outward change—in our garments, in our autos, in our prepping—may feel vital, yet is shallow in contrast to the internal change. That is the genuine change we have to concentrate on. Remember Seneca's recommendation: "Internally, we should be distinctive in each regard, yet our outward dress should mix in with the group."

18. Go out for a Stroll — Throughout the ages, rationalists, scholars, writers, and masterminds have discovered that strolling offers an extra advantage—time and space for better work. As Nietzsche would later say: "It is just thoughts picked up from strolling that have any worth." Or here is Seneca: "We should take meandering outside strolls, with the goal that the brain may be sustained and invigorated by the outdoors and profound relaxing."

19. Try not to Be Ashamed To Ask For Help — "Don't be embarrassed about requiring help. You have an obligation to satisfy simply like a trooper on the mass of fight. So imagine a scenario where you are harmed and cannot ascend without another warrior's assistance?" Marcus Aurelius.

20. Carry out Your Job — In his Meditations, Marcus Aurelius asks himself: "What is your business?" He at that point answers: "To be a decent individual." The Stoics accepted, regardless of anything else, that our employment on this planet is to be a decent person. It is a fundamental obligation, yet we are specialists at thinking of reasons for keeping away from it. As mentor Bill Belichick put it: "Carry out your occupation."

CONCLUSION

In conclusion, Stoicism might be an ancient philosophy that draws a lot of misconceptions towards it, but as we have noted in the book, we can learn a lot and employ it in our day to day lives. It is not a philosophy about emotionlessness but rather endurance and simplicity.

We could borrow from one of its three principal leaders on how to endure hardship and translate that into our lives. In this book, we have covered important ideas that include understanding emotions and how to be calm in chaos. These concepts are all borrowed and are derivatives of Stoic teachings and the philosophy in general.

We certainly hope that this book shall shed much-needed light on this very misunderstood philosophy that dates quite a while back. Likewise, we intend for it to not only provide a good read but also lead you to live a much-fulfilled life through its input on contemporary life.

There, of course, are a lot of other books that decipher this ancient philosophy that is Stoicism and provide a good insight into it. It is time for you to create a structure in your life, a mentality of strength and a maturity in emotions. We are all liable to change, things happen in our lives that can make us give up on life. We hope that this book has given you the right skills, and ideas for you to approach life with a better meaning and understanding that is far greater than you had imagined.

Made in the USA
San Bernardino, CA
30 August 2017